Malaysia and Singapore

Malaysia, a federation of thirteen states, occupies two distinct regions: Peninsular Malaysia, stretching from the border of Thailand to the Straits of Johore; and Sabah and Sarawak on the northwestern coast of the Island of Borneo (or Kalimantan). Separating the two areas is about 750 km (466 miles) of the South China Sea.

The Republic of Singapore, once part of Malaysia, has been an independent city-state since 1965. It comprises one main island and 54 smaller ones. Singapore lies at the southern tip of the Malay Peninsula, about half a mile from the mainland, to which it is linked by a causeway.

The people of Malaysia and Singapore are of different ethnic origins, the three main races being the Malays (and other native peoples), the Chinese and the Indians. Together they have worked to make their nations an economic success.

The Malaysian economy is still dependent on agriculture, but manufacturing industries are being encouraged by the government. Singapore's wealth has centered around its harbor, one of the largest and busiest in the world. But in the last decade, manufacturing industries, such as microelectronics and textiles, have begun to play an important part.

In *We live in Malaysia & Singapore*, a cross section of the people of both nations tell you what their life is like.

Jessie Wee lives in Singapore, where she is a well-known author of children's books.

Malaysian-born Chuah Ai Mee helped her produce this book.

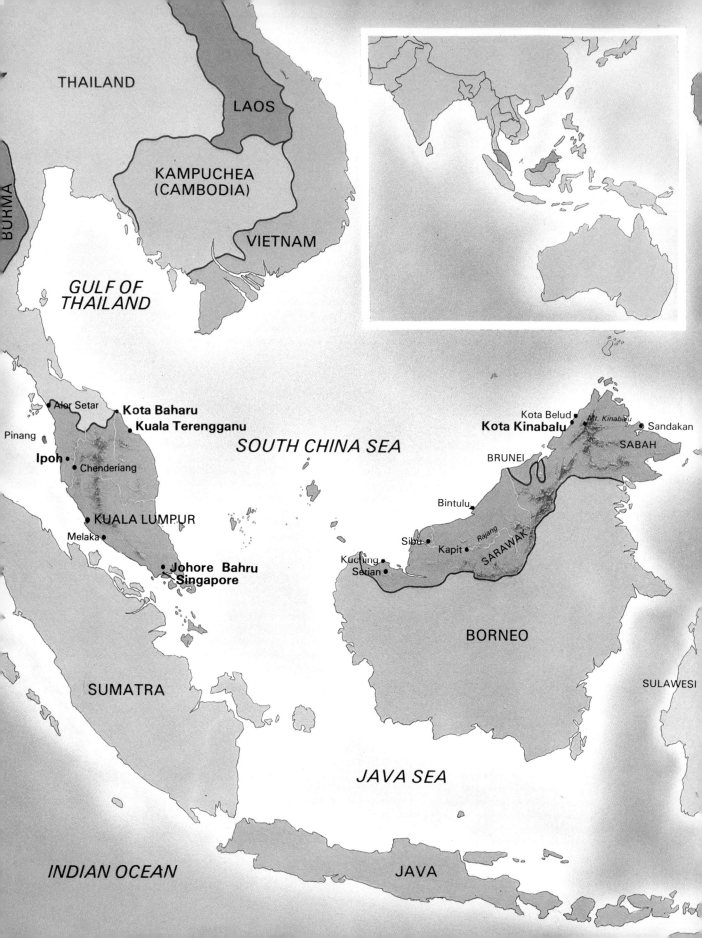

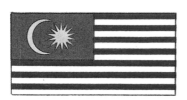

we live in
MALAYSIA
&
SINGAPORE

Jessie Wee

The Bookwright Press
New York · 1985

Living Here

We live in Argentina
We live in Brazil
We live in Britain
We live in Canada
We live in the Caribbean
We live in Chile
We live in China
We live in Denmark
We live in France
We live in Greece
We live in India
We live in Israel

We live in Italy
We live in Japan
We live in Kenya
We live in Malaysia & Singapore
We live in New Zealand
We live in Pakistan
We live in South Africa
We live in Spain
We live in Sweden
We live in the Asian U.S.S.R.
We live in the European U.S.S.R.
We live in West Germany

First published in the United States in 1985 by
The Bookwright Press, 387 Park Avenue South,
New York, NY 10016

First published in 1984 by
Wayland (Publishers) Ltd
49 Lansdowne Place, Hove
East Sussex BN3 1HF, England

© Copyright 1984 Wayland (Publishers) Ltd
All rights reserved
ISBN 0−531−18007−7
Library of Congress Catalog Card Number: 84−73585

Printed by G. Canale & C.S.p.A., Turin, Italy

Contents

"The melting pot of various cultures"

Safarinah Abdul Rahim is a Malay folk dancer who lives in Singapore. She and her husband have spent many years promoting Malay dance. With their Rina Dance Group, they hope to create their own uniquely Singaporean style of Malay dance and drama.

When Stamford Raffles of the British East India Company first came to Singapore, in 1819, he found a swampy island covered with dense jungle. Tigers roamed the land and pirates the sea. The only inhabitants were about a hundred Malays who had come to settle at the mouth of the Singapore River and a handful of Chinese growing pepper and gambier.

Today, Singapore is a busy, bustling city-state of skyscrapers. It has a multi-racial population of almost 2.5 million. Many are descendants of immigrants who came from China, the Malay Peninsula and India. Out of this racial and cultural background has emerged a uniquely Singaporean identity.

New trends, new traits, new values have appeared over the years and, partly because of education and the influx of western influences, various aspects of our different cultures have undergone tremendous changes. Singapore has become the melting pot of various cultures, so much so that in dance, as in other forms of art, we are becoming distinctly Singaporean.

I'm particularly interested in dance. For me, dancing is an expression of the joy of

The Rina Dance Group performs "Payang": a dance to welcome fishermen back from a trip.

"Ratu": a dance about a queen who brings peace and prosperity to her kingdom.

living, the joy of being Singaporean. In promoting Malay dance, I'm trying to preserve my cultural heritage. Yet in trying to create my own style and break away from the traditional form, I'm trying to express myself as a Singaporean.

I've been dancing since the age of 5, and have had no formal training.

At the age of 15, I joined the *Perkumpulan Seni*, a Malay dance group in Singapore. I performed with this group for six years. During this time, too, I was a dancer in the newly formed National Dance Company, established by the Ministry of Culture in 1972. Singapore wanted to keep its cultural traditions and at the same time create its own local style.

I've been with the National Dance Company ever since and have performed both locally and abroad, in places as far away as the U.S., Iran, Belgium, and Korea.

In 1975, my husband and I formed our own Rina Dance Group to give ourselves more scope in creating and establishing our own Singaporean style of dance and dance drama. My husband is the choreographer and I help to design the costumes. Besides using taped music, we've started experimenting with live music, using Malay drums, like the *rebana* and the *gendang*, gongs and other more modern musical instruments.

Our Chinese and Indian friends, too, have joined our group, giving our performance a truly multiracial flavor. What makes me most happy is to see our young Singaporeans of various races dancing together and enjoying themselves.

"Mount Kinabalu is a sacred mountain"

Yaakub bin Dikam, 18, is a trainee wood-carver at the Malaysian handicraft center in Kota Belud, a small town 77 km (48 miles) north of Kota Kinabalu, in Sabah. He lives in a small village, Kampung Lingkodon, just outside Kota Belud.

In just a few months' I will have completed my sixteen-month course at the handicraft training center. Then I shall start my own little business at home: making such things as letter racks, mirror frames, walking sticks, and clocks.

I'll sell them at our *tamu* (open-air Sunday market) in Kota Belud.

Besides wood carving, the center has classes in *kain songket* (cloth) weaving, *buloh* (bamboo) weaving, *pandan* (screw-pine-leaf) weaving and rattan craft. There are 52 student-trainees at the center, from all over Sabah.

The boys usually sign up for wood carving or rattan craft. The girls are more interested in *kain songket* and *pandan* weaving. *Buloh* weaving usually attracts both sexes.

This center is the only one of its kind in the whole of Sabah. But to encourage native handicrafts, the state government is planning to open another one in Tambunan, about 80 km (50 miles) southeast of Kota Kinabalu.

Sarawak also has only one handicraft training center. It is in Kuching. Peninsular Malaysia has several dotted around it.

I'm a Bajau, the largest native group in Sabah after the Kadazans. Many tribal groups make up our Bajau community. They include the Illanun, Suluk, Obian, Binadan and Bajau peoples who originally came from the southern Philippines in the eighteenth and early nineteenth centuries. Most of us are Moslems, although some Bajaus have become Christians.

The Bajaus are seafaring people. Their skill in handicrafts can be seen in the elaborate carvings on their fishing boats. Nowadays, many Bajaus have turned to cattle farming and growing rice. The largest concentration of Bajaus can be found in the foothills of Mount Kinabalu, especially in our Kota Belud area which is famous for its Bajau "cowboys." They are an impressive sight when they dress up in their traditional costumes and ride their gaily decorated horses on festive occasions.

A view of the foothills of Mount Kinabalu, the highest mountain in the whole of Malaysia.

I can't ride a horse because my aunt and uncle, who brought me up, are rice growers, and they have never owned any horses or cattle; but some of our neighbors in Kampung Lingkodon do keep them.

Our *kampung* (village) is about 10 km (6 miles) from Kota Belud. To reach our village you have to take a pick-up truck out of town. Then there's a longish walk from the road and finally a suspension bridge over a river to cross. Kampung Lingkodon is a quiet, lovely village with wooden houses built on stilts.

Beyond our rice fields and cattle-grazing lands rise the foothills of our famous Mount Kinabalu. Mount Kinabalu, at 4,101 m (13,455 feet), is the highest mountain in Malaysia. Many of our people regard it as a sacred mountain for they believe it is the resting place of the dead.

Yaakub and some of the other students in his woodworking class at the handicraft center.

"My parents chose my husband"

Ee Kit Neo is a Straits Chinese *Nyonya* (woman). Her way of life is the result of the combination of two different cultures. She is 90 years old and lives in Melaka with her youngest son.

Do you know where Melaka is? Do you also know that it's the oldest town in Malaysia? It has ruins and buildings that date back to the times when the Portuguese ruled, in the sixteenth century. It also has some of the finest old-style Chinese houses to be seen in Malaysia.

I was born in Melaka on November 13, 1893. At that time Pinang, Melaka and Singapore were ruled by the British. They were known as the Straits Settlements.

A Straits Chinese bride and groom in their heavily-embroidered wedding outfits.

The early Chinese immigrants to these areas adopted part of the language and culture of the Malays. But they didn't give up their own customs and traditions. The result was the birth of a new culture – the *Peranakan* or Straits Chinese culture.

The *Peranakan* men are known as *Babas* and the women as *Nyonyas*. The early Melaka *Babas* wore long jackets, loose trousers and black skullcaps like their counterparts in China. Their descendants, though, switched to European dress in the late nineteenth century. They could be identified from the other Chinese only by their speech and mannerisms. The *Babas* speak little or no Chinese, but *Baba* Malay. Those with an English education speak English.

The *Nyonyas* like myself wear a *sarung*, (loose ankle-length skirt) like the Malay women. With it, I wear the *kebaya* (blouse) which is fastened in front by three diamond brooches. My granddaughters no longer dress this way. They wear modern clothes.

I had a very strict upbringing. I was taught to sweep, dust, cook and sew. I wasn't allowed to step out of the house. Nor could I play games with my brothers. When I was caught doing so, I was severely punished. My playmates could only be my sisters or female cousins.

Life was so different when I was a young girl. There were no automobiles, so visits to relatives on special occasions, like birthdays, weddings and the Chinese New Year, were made in sedan chairs or in carriages drawn by horses or bullocks.

I married at 18. My parents chose my husband for me. By then, I could sew, make cakes and cook *Nyonya* food, which is pungent and spicy like Malay and Indian food. I also knew how to arrange and prepare offerings for the ancestral altar. We offer food and drinks in honor of our ancestors. We also have an altar at home where offerings are made to Buddha and deities like the Kitchen God and *Kuan Yin*, the Goddess of Mercy.

My elaborate wedding ceremony lasted for twelve days. The groom and I were dressed in the heavily embroidered Straits Chinese wedding robes and met for the first time at the ceremony.

After marriage, I came under the control of my mother-in-law. I still wasn't allowed to go out freely, even with my husband. Nevertheless, we had a long and happy marriage and were blessed with four sons and six daughters.

I brought my children up in the Straits Chinese tradition. Of course, as time went on, things changed. Ceremonies were simplified and many of our customs were no longer practiced.

We still celebrate the Chinese New Year, though. It's a very important day for us.

I still prepare the *ang pow* (red packets with money in them). These I give to the children and all unmarried people who come to pay their respects to me during the New Year season.

Ee Kit Neo with two of the ang pow *which she gives to unmarried people at New Year.*

"25 percent of the world's tin"

Leong Fah works in the Foong Seong mine at Chenderiang, 48 km (30 miles) south of Ipoh. He is 72 years old. Born in China, he has been working in Perak State's tin mines since 1930.

Everyone looks surprised when I say I'm 72. But I am – a very fit and healthy 72. That's because I've led an outdoor life ever since I was 18. A very hard, tough life as a tin-mine worker in the Kinta Valley in the state of Perak.

Mention Kinta Valley and everyone in Malaysia thinks of tin. This area of about 1,800 sq km (700 sq miles) contains rich, alluvial deposits of tin ore. It has the largest concentration of tin mines in the country and produces almost 50 percent of Malaysia's tin. Another 25 percent comes from the state of Selangor to the south and the rest from a few other states in Peninsular Malaysia.

Thousands of Chinese immigrants flocked to these rich, tin-mining areas in the 1850s. Today, old mining camps, like Ipoh and Kuala Lumpur, are busy, prosperous cities.

Malaysia produces almost 25 percent of the world's tin. It is found in lodes in the central mountain ranges of the peninsula. Much of the tin, though, has been washed

down from the mountains and deposited in the foothills.

Large companies use dredgers which can dig to a depth of 40 m (130 feet) below the surface of the lake on which they float.

But most Chinese tin miners prefer the gravel pump. I've worked in opencast mines which use the gravel-pump method ever since I came to Malaysia in 1930.

In gravel pumping, powerful jets of water from a narrow pipe, called a monitor, are trained on the sides of an opencast mine. The water washes the alluvium into a sump at the bottom of the mine. The gravel, containing the tin ore, is then pumped up a pipe to the top of a tall, sloping wooden structure. The larger stones are trapped at the top of the structure while the small stones, sand and clay are washed down the sluice box *(palong)*. Low bars of wood at intervals of 1.5 m (5 feet) trap the heavy tin concentrates while the waste material flows off the end of the *palong*.

The water is not wasted, because it is

diverted back to the pumps and used again. Sometimes, women *dulang* washers can be found at the foot of the *palong*. They use pans called *dulangs* to catch any tin ore that may have escaped. The *dulang* and *palong* are two very old methods that have survived to this day.

The tin concentrates are sent to Piṅang, Butterworth and Klang where they are smelted and turned into ingots of tin. The U.S., the U.S.S.R., Japan and the E.E.C. (European Economic Community) are the main buyers of Malaysian tin.

When I was young, there were more gravel pumps and dredgers in operation. There are fewer today because the output of tin has dropped. So have tin prices.

I've seen a lot of changes in my time, having worked in tin mines for fifty-four years. I don't know when I'll retire. I've been too busy to think about that!

A dulang *washer uses a pan to catch any tin ore washed down from the* palong (sluice box).

Powerful jets of water from a "monitor" are trained on the sides of the opencast mine.

"There's no electricity in our quarters"

Born in India, Thangam Muthusamy, 42, works as a tea picker on the Boh Tea Plantation near Tanah Rata, the principal village in the mountain resort of Cameron Highlands in Peninsular Malaysia. She is married and has three children.

My parents brought me to Peninsular Malaysia from India at the age of 4. At 15 I married, according to Hindu custom, and left the lowlands of Perak for the mountain resort of Cameron Highlands, in the nearby state of Pahang. My husband and I found work as tea pluckers on a plantation near Tanah Rata. We've worked here for more than twenty years now.

It's hot and humid in the lowlands with temperatures around 27°C (80°F). Here, at 1,500 m (5,000 feet) above sea level, the weather is cool, with average day temperatures of about 21°C (70°F). Night temperatures can drop to 16°C (60°F) or lower.

When I first came here, I knew nothing about the place. Friends soon told me it was named after a government surveyor, William Cameron. In 1925, it was decided to develop this area, which was then covered with dense rain forest. Plans for tea estates and towns were drawn up and a mountain road constructed.

Farmers soon discovered that the climate was excellent for growing flowers, cabbage, lettuce, tomatoes and other vegetables. They came to cultivate the valley floors and lower mountain slopes.

After being picked, the tea leaves are inspected and put into large sacks and weighed.

Today, fresh flowers and vegetables are supplied to Singapore and to local markets all over Peninsular Malaysia.

Over the years, Cameron Highlands has developed into a popular mountain resort. Malaysians and tourists come to enjoy the cool, temperate climate and the beautiful mountain scenery.

The tea shrubs grow very well on the cool, wet and well-drained mountain slopes. Most of the tea grown in this area, and on the coastal plains of Selangor, is for local consumption but some of it is exported to neighboring countries, like Singapore and Brunei.

Our plantation, the largest in Malaysia, covers an area of 760 hectares (1,900 acres). It produces over 1.5 million kg (3 million lb) of tea annually. The variety of tea grown here came originally from Assam in northeast India. Grown from either seeds or cuttings, tea shrubs can be plucked in the third year, then up to the sixtieth year and beyond.

The tea shrubs are pruned to a height of 1.5 m (5 ft). The young, tender leaves are picked throughout the year, with fields being worked in rotation so that the shrubs are picked once every ten days.

I work a six-day week, from 8 a.m. to 4 p.m., with Sundays off. By 11 a.m., the basket strapped to my back is full and heavy. I walk down the narrow, twisting mountain road to the shed some distance away. Here, the leaves are inspected, then put into sacks and weighed. The weight is recorded in a book next to my name.

After an hour's break for lunch, I start work again. I can pluck an average of 50 kg (110 lb) of tea leaves per day and earn about M$300 (U.S.$125) per month. This is spent on food, clothes and necessities. My living quarters are provided free.

There's no electricity in our quarters, so we use either firewood or bottled gas for our cooking. Our homes are lighted by paraffin lamps.

Thangam at work on the Boh Tea Plantation, in Cameron Highlands.

"We go to school from Sunday to Thursday"

Fathiyah is 12 and her brother, Fauzi, is 10. They both go to elementary school. They live in Alor Setar, the capital of the rice-growing state of Kedah, in the northwestern part of Peninsular Malaysia.

Fathiyah: My name is Fathiyah binte Haji Salleh Hilmi. *Binte* in Malay means "daughter of." My father has the title *Haji* before his name because he has been on a pilgrimage to Mecca.

All my friends call me Iyah. I'm in my sixth year of elementary school or *Darjah 6* as it's called in Malaysia. School starts at 7:45 a.m. and finishes at 1:25 p.m.

We're taught in Malay. It's our national language. We also learn English as a second language. I enjoy my language classes and when I grow up I want to be a teacher like my father. My other favorite subjects are mathematics and history. We have music, art and physical education classes, too.

Not all the Moslem girls in my school dress the way I do. Most of them wear a blouse and jumper. I wear a *baju kurong* (loose blouse and *sarung*) and a *mini telekong* (headdress) because my family prefers to follow this style of dress.

My home is about 3 km (2 miles) from school and I've been bicycling to and from school ever since I was 9. When my brother was younger, he sat quietly behind me.

Parents picking up their children from school at the end of the morning session.

Now, he too wants to bicycle to school. So we take turns.

After school, I usually help my mother at home – cooking, sweeping the house or washing dishes. Sometimes, I help look after my baby sister who is just over a year old.

When I'm free, I like to play with the dolls that I made myself from pieces of cloth. I like to play house. I think it's fun.

Fauzi: Like Iyah, I have a very long name. It's Mohammad Fauzi bin Haji Salleh Hilmi. *Bin* in Malay means "son of." My name is also written as Mohd Fauzi. My friends, of course, call me Fauzi. So does the family.

Did you know we go to school from Sunday to Thursday? All schools in Kedah close on Friday and Saturday. This is because we're a Moslem state and Friday is our day of prayer. My father, big brother, younger brother and I go to the mosque near my school from 12:30 p.m. to 2:00 p.m. to pray every Friday. My mother and sisters do not join us at prayer. They

Across the road from the playground is the mosque which Fauzi goes to every Friday.

usually go to a smaller mosque near our home with the other women.

I'm in my fourth year at school. My favorite subject is geography. I like to study about people in other lands. When I'm big enough I want to be a pilot. Then I can travel to countries all over the world.

In geography, we learn that Kedah is the most important rice-growing state in Peninsular Malaysia. Unfortunately, the rice we grow is not enough to feed our people. We have to buy rice from Thailand and Burma. We eat rice every day. It's our staple food.

My favorite sports are soccer and badminton. I like to play with my friends who live near me. I don't like playing badminton with my big brother because he always wins!

I like to play soccer with Iyah. She's very good. She can kick the ball very well but she doesn't like to play with me because she says I'm very rough.

"Malaysia's cloth of gold"

Aisah binte Rahman lives on the east coast of Peninsular Malaysia. Born in Kota Baharu, capital of the state of Kelantan, she works as a *kain songket* weaver in Penumbang on the outskirts of the city.

The *kain songket*, Malaysia's "cloth of gold (cloth embroidered with gold thread)," has been in use since the fifteenth century. At that time, it was made by the weavers of the Malay royal courts.

In the olden days, *kain songket* weaving was a closely guarded secret that was passed from mother to daughter down through the generations. But today, any girl or woman, who is bright and persistent enough, can learn to weave it.

I was only 10 when I first learned to weave the *kain songket*. It took me about a week to master the huge, wooden, traditional handloom which has not changed with time. Some girls take a month, some a year and some never at all!

I work at Cik Minah's shop in Penumbang, on the outskirts of Kota Baharu. Situated beside the road which leads to *Pantai Chinta Berahi* (Beach of Passionate Love), you'll find Cik Minah's shop along with many other family-run businesses which make *kain songket, batik* (patterned, dyed cloth), *wau* (kites) and other handicrafts for which the east coast of Peninsular Malaysia is famous.

The handlooms at Cik Minah's are set up under the house, which is built on stilts. In the house itself is the shop where the *kain songket* and other local handicrafts are displayed.

I have my own handloom at home and often work on my own pieces when I'm free. So do many housewives who cannot work a full week.

Kain songket weaving is a thriving cottage industry on the east coast. The women in the states of Kelantan and Terengganu are famous throughout Malaysia for their fine, exquisite work.

Prices for each *kain songket* can range from M$80 to $500 (U.S.$30–$200), depending on whether cotton or silk threads are used for the main body of the fabric. Prices also depend on the quality of the gold thread used for the decorative pattern on the fabric. These threads are imported from India.

The main body of the *kain songket*

In outfits made of kain songket, *a Malay bride and groom are escorted to their wedding.*

comes in one single plain color – such as light blue, deep blue, red, maroon, green, purple, or yellow.

Malay men and women from all levels of society wear the *kain songket* at ceremonial functions, and it is a *must* at weddings. Traditional wedding costumes worn by Malay brides and grooms throughout Malaysia and Singapore are made of *kain songket*.

Today's designers, too, have fashioned the *kain songket* into evening gowns. You can also find scarves and stoles and decorative wall hangings all made of Malaysia's lovely *kain songket*.

The bride and groom sit on a dais during a Malay wedding ceremony.

"Orangutans are in danger of becoming extinct"

Lawrence Singah, 37, is a game warden at the Orangutan Rehabilitation Center in Sepilok, 24 km (15 miles) from Sandakan, in the state of Sabah. The orangutan is one of the thirty-five protected species in Malaysia.

This center is the only one of its kind in the world. On the edge of the Sepilok Forest Reserve in east Sabah, we rescue orangutans (literally meaning "man of the forest") from hunters and teach them to live in the wild again.

I also check on reports of the illegal keeping of orangutans or any other protected wildlife such as gibbons, monkeys, turtles or hornbills. I also help to catch people hunting these endangered species. People who are caught can be fined up to M$5,000 (U.S.$2,000), and given a five-year prison sentence.

Orangutans are found in Sabah, Borneo and Sumatra. Sabah has the largest number of them – over 3,000. But orangutans are a species which is in danger of becoming extinct. The main reason for this is the timber industry: cutting down trees has forced the orangutans into the mountainous regions where they cannot find enough fruit, leaves or bark to feed on.

They're also easy victims of hunters because they're curious animals who aren't afraid of people. When approached, they don't run away. The young, helpless orangutans are often captured by hunters, who kill their mothers.

Sam helps himself to the fresh green grass while Lawrence stands by with a second helping.

The part of the work I like best is supervising the rehabilitation of the lovable orangutan babies rescued from hunters. We help them to adjust to living in the forests again.

What we try to do is help these young orangutans find food, build tree-nests, climb trees and become so independent that they will go out to live in the wild. Since the Center was set up, in 1964, we have succeeded in releasing more than a hundred orangutans back to their natural habitat in the forest.

Baby orangutans are delicate and totally dependent on others for their food and care. They're also prone to human infections. They become more independent when they're about five years old.

Most of the animals in our center are young, orphaned orangutans, but we look after other animals, as well, like honey-bears, hornbills, storks and monkeys.

At the moment, we're looking after a baby elephant who was found wandering alone in the forest. He had somehow got separated from his mother and herd. We call him Sam. We hope to release him in the forest by finding a herd of elephants who will "adopt" him.

A barrowful of trouble? Young orangutans wait to be taken to their exercise area at the Center.

"Skyscrapers are unavoidable in Singapore"

Lim Kit Chia, 38, is a director of Eng Hup Heng Construction, a building company involved in both residential and industrial projects in Singapore. He has worked in the building industry since the age of 20.

Singaporeans who return from living overseas blink in astonishment at the changing skyline of their tiny island state. High-rise apartment buildings, hotels, shopping centers, banks, offices, factories and schools seem to have mushroomed all over the island during their absence.

Towering skyscrapers are unavoidable in land-hungry Singapore. With a population of 2.5 million people, a land area of only 618 sq km (239 sq miles) and a population density of almost 4,000 persons per sq km (10,360 people per sq mile), high-rise living has become a way of life.

Construction work has speeded up since 1979, resulting in a building boom that has contributed greatly to the growth of Singapore's economy. The Housing and Development Board, a government body, provides about 75 percent of the people with well-planned, subsidized housing. It builds apartments which are four to five times cheaper than those erected by private firms.

I joined the construction industry in the early sixties at the age of 20. I worked my way up through various jobs, learning as I went along. Then in the early seventies I formed a building company with a group of friends. We have never looked back since. We've won many building contracts for residential and industrial projects in Singapore from both the government and private firms.

When I started in this industry, most of my fellow construction workers were Singaporeans. Today, because of the rapid expansion of the industry and the attraction of other jobs, there is an acute shortage of workers. To meet our labor needs, we've had to recruit large numbers of people from Malaysia, Thailand, Sri Lanka and Macao.

My challenging job has given me a great deal of satisfaction. When I drive past the places my workers and I have helped build, I cannot help but feel proud.

(Right) With limited land available for building, Singapore is certainly on the up-and-up!

"Seas warm and rich in plankton"

Abu Bakar bin Ali is a fisherman. He is 43 and lives in a fishing village not far from the mouth of the Terengganu River. The state of Terengganu, where he lives, is famous for its fishing, handicrafts and offshore oil.

When I was a child, my elders always said, "To be a good fisherman, you must be both brave and smart: brave enough to face the unpredictable sea and weather in your boat, and smart enough to know where the different types of fish can be found."

And I had thought how very true this was, especially in the past when fishing on the east coast of Peninsular Malaysia was carried out in small sailing boats manned by only a few men. Today, life is easier because, with government assistance, we can afford to buy outboard motors and even boats with all the very latest fishing equipment.

I have a medium-sized boat which I bought with an interest-free loan from the government. I operate it with the help of three other men from my fishing village. The money we earn from each day's catch is divided among the four of us after expenses for food, oil and the government loan are deducted.

A lot of fishing is done in Malaysia, which is surrounded by water. Because of the Sunda Shelf, the seas around Malaysia

Fishermen selling their day's catch to dealers who will transport it all over Terengganu state.

Abu Bakar prepares for another trip.

are quite shallow, and the water warm and rich in plankton on which the fish feed.

Fish is plentiful and many fishermen can be found on the east coast of Peninsular Malaysia, with the largest number in the state of Terengganu where I live. But in spite of this, more fish are caught off the west coast of Peninsular Malaysia.

This is because our fishing boats cannot go out to the South China Sea during the northeast monsoon which blows from October to February. The sea is too rough. The Malacca Strait off the west coast, on the other hand, is well sheltered and free from violent storms.

My home is the fishing village of Kampung Losong Masjid, about 3 km (2 miles) from Kuala Terengganu, the state capital. Our homes are simple wooden huts, built on stilts.

Life in the fishing villages of Terengganu has not changed much over the years. When the men are out at sea, the women look after the children and attend to all the household chores. Those who have time to spare make baskets, mats and other ornamental articles from *pandan* or *mengkuang* (different varieties of screw-pine leaves). Some of the women weave the *kain songket* (cloth embroidered with gold thread) or do other handicrafts for which the east coast is famous.

My wife hardly has any time to spare. She's too busy looking after our nine children, four of whom are still at school.

"My 4 brothers, 7 sisters and I were born here"

Rasoo Ramasamy, 52, is a spice merchant. His shop is in Serangoon Road, an area known today as Singapore's "Little India." Indians form about 6.4 percent of Singapore's population.

Two of my brothers and I are still carrying on the business which our father started in 1931. Born in India, he came to Singapore as a young man to look for work. He married and settled here and saved up enough money to open a shop. My four brothers, seven sisters and I were born here.

Our shop is open from 8:00 a.m. to 8:00 p.m. every day except Sunday. We have a staff of eight, including a cook, because we provide our workers with room and board. They are either Indian Moslems or Hindus and live above the shop.

Besides spices, we also sell medicinal herbs, grinding-stones which housewives use to grind their spices, earthenware pots, incense sticks, pickles, rose water, sandlewood powder, perfumes and other things which Indian families need for their cooking, as well as for their religious festivals, weddings and other ceremonies. We import many of these items from India. We make our own curry powder, too!

Our shop is in the part of Serangoon Road known as Singapore's "Little India." It's the very heart of Singapore's Indian

A Hindu devotee carries a kavadi *during the* Thaipusam *procession.*

There's hardly any room for customers in Rasoo's spice shop in Serangoon Road!

community. Singapore Indians can find anything they need in this road. Shops lining both sides of the road in the Indian sector sell everything from spices, provisions, jewelry and clothes to flowers, books and statues of all the Hindu gods. Here one finds the Indian barbers, tailors, money lenders, and astrologers, too.

During the religious festival of *Thaipusam*, which usually falls in January, half of Serangoon Road is closed to traffic. This is to allow a procession to take place. To fulfill vows of thanksgiving and penance, several thousand Hindu devotees pierce their bodies with spears and skewers. To the sound of chants and beating drums, they walk from the temple in Serangoon Road to the temple in Tank Road.

My family and I go to both temples to pray and to bring offerings of flowers. We also walk with friends or relatives who take part in the procession.

After *Thaipusam*, everything returns to normal and the Indian shops that close for the day re-open for business. Singaporeans and tourists visit Serangoon Road again to shop, sightsee or eat at the Indian restaurants that are famous for their southern Indian dishes. The food is rich, chili hot – and full of our spices.

"Kadazans are a very musical people"

Twenty-five-year-old Jovina Laban is a stewardess with the Malaysian Airline System, whose initials MAS mean gold in the national language. She is a Kadazan and comes from Kota Kinabalu, capital of the state of Sabah.

"Come and join us, Jovina. You'll love working in MAS, meeting people and traveling. Besides, you'll be getting much more than what you're earning now. Think about it while we get the application forms for you."

That was how persistent my friends were. Anyhow, I was ready for a change. I was bored with my job. So I resigned and at the age of 22 joined our national airline. Then I was sent to Kuala Lumpur for training. I passed both the practical and written examinations with flying colors and went back to Kota Kinabalu to begin work as a stewardess.

I spent five months serving on Fokker Friendship aircraft, flying to the main towns throughout Sabah and Sarawak. After that, I was based in Kuala Lumpur where I spent a year serving on Boeing 737s, flying to places throughout Peninsular Malaysia as well as to Singapore, Medan, Jakarta, Manila and Bangkok.

I'm now working on the Airbus and DC-10 planes which fly to such destinations as Perth, Madras and Jeddah. In just a few months I shall be flying on Boeing 747s on the route to London and Europe. I'm very excited about it as I've never been so far afield.

MAS has a fleet of 34 aircraft. It flies to 22 major cities in Europe, Asia and Australia, besides providing air links to 36 domestic destinations.

Recently, I took part in *Bakat MAS*, a staff talent show which is held annually. I sang a solo and was delighted when I won the competition.

Singing comes naturally to me. We Kadazans are a very musical people. We love to sing and dance to the music of our flutes and the beat of our gongs. I've been singing in school concerts ever since I was 10. By the age of 16 I was appearing on Sabah TV as a singer.

I sing in English and love the blues, jazz and rock. I was taught in English. I'm fluent in Malay, our national language, and can also speak Kadazan and Hakka, a Chinese dialect I learned from my mother.

Passengers boarding an MAS Airbus aircraft. It flies to such places as Jeddah and Madras.

We are Christians. Not all Kadazans are Christians, though. Some are Moslems, while others still observe their ancestral customs and traditions. But the Kadazans form the largest native group in Sabah. Now, whenever there are weddings and festivals to celebrate, we put on our traditional Kadazan costumes. These are wonderful occasions and I never miss them if I can help it. Whenever I'm on leave, I fly back to Kota Kinabalu where my parents live.

Some of MAS's fleet of 34 aircraft at Kuala Lumpur's international airport.

"Land is scarce . . . intensive farming is necessary"

Low Hee Tang is a florist. He is a first-generation Singaporean and is helping his father run the family's nursery and flower shops. He is 25, a bachelor and the youngest son in a family of nine.

My father started the nursery and my grandfather, when he was alive, used to help him. They were both born in China. My three brothers, five sisters and I were all born in Singapore.

I went to a Chinese school and I'm fluent in Mandarin, but I can speak English as it was my second language in school. After my national service (which is compulsory in Singapore for all able-bodied male citizens when they reach the age of 18), I joined the family business. I'm now in charge of our main flower shop in the Katong district.

Our family home is in Changi. I live there with my parents, some of my brothers and sisters and their children. Ours is a three-generation family living together: a way of life which is rapidly disappearing in modern Singapore, but which our government is now actively encouraging.

Home is a wooden bungalow on stilts as our Chinese *kampung* (village) is often flooded, especially when it rains heavily and the tide is high. Most of my neighbors in this rural district live in huts made of light timber with *attap* (palm thatch) or zinc roofs. They own small

There is a tremendous demand for flowers during the Chinese New Year celebrations.

vegetable plots where mustard *(Cai xin)*, Chinese kale *(Gai lan)*, broccoli and cauliflower are grown. These are sold to local housewives at vegetable stalls in the market. Unfortunately, supply doesn't meet demand, so about 75 percent of our vegetables have to be imported from Cameron Highlands in Peninsular Malaysia, China, Australia and other countries.

Only about 11 percent of the land area in Singapore is used for agricultural purposes. As land is scarce in our densely populated island, intensive farming is necessary. We have pig farming in Ponggol, hydroponic farming in Bah Soon Pah Road, orchid and flower nurseries in Jalan Kayu and mushroom farming and fish breeding farms in other areas. My family will soon be relocated to another part of Singapore to make way for new houses and factories in our part of Changi.

Our nursery in Changi is small – less than 1 hectare (2½ acres). We grow and sell potted plants, like orchids, roses, bougainvilleas, ferns and crotons. We also sell fertilizers, flower pots, various types of soil, imported packages of flower seeds and all kinds of gardening tools from the U.S., Japan, Taiwan, China and Britain.

Our flower shops sell cut flowers, mostly imported from Cameron Highlands, Thailand, Taiwan, Australia and Holland.

The demand for flowers increases tremendously during festive seasons, and if you live in multiracial Singapore you'll know that the Chinese have their New Year, the Malays their *Hari Raya* and the Indians their *Deepavali*. Then, there is Christmas as well as festivals celebrated by the other races in Singapore.

Our busiest time is the Chinese New Year – the season for lion dances and big family dinners.

Hee Tang in his family's nursery in Changi, where a variety of potted plants are grown.

"Timber is a big money-maker for Sabah"

Omat bin Gajah, 34, is a worker at the Lungmanis Timber Camp, about 80 km (50 miles) west of the port of Sandakan, in the state of Sabah. Timber is an important industry in the state.

Kuamut is a little village on the banks of the Kinabatangan River in the interior of Sabah. I was born in Kuamut and belong to a small group of native people known as the *Orang Sungai*, meaning "People of the River." We live by fishing, growing rice, vegetables and corn, as well as by hunting.

About five years ago, I started working in lumber camps near my village. The pay was good and so I moved from camp to camp to find whatever work I could get. As all lumber camps provided free living quarters, I brought my wife and three children along with me.

In 1983, I started at the Lungmanis Timber Camp. My job is to operate a crane that lowers logs into the Klapis River that flows nearby.

My fellow timber workers in the forest use chain saws to cut down the trees. After the branches have been lopped off, the logs are hauled through the forest to the road by a caterpillar tractor. There, they are loaded onto a truck and brought to a field on the banks of the Klapis River.

Now I take over, using my crane to lift log after log and release them into the river

A truck transporting logs to the banks of a nearby river for floating downstream.

below. There they are tied together and towed downriver to a "log pond" in Sandakan.

A log pond is simply an area of water fenced in with logs which trap the logs brought down from here.

In a log pond, the logs are sorted and graded, ready for export to countries like Japan, South Korea and Taiwan. Most of Sabah's timber is exported in the form of logs. Some, however, is sent to sawmills to be made into planks or plywood.

The timber industry is a big moneymaker for Sabah and, in fact, for the whole of Malaysia. In recent years, timber has become Malaysia's second largest earner of foreign currency – about 15 percent of export earnings. Peninsular Malaysia produces about 90 percent of the sawed timber, while Sabah and Sarawak produce about 64 percent of the total output of logs. Most of the timber is cut down in forest areas which are under the government's control. It keeps an eye on things so that our forests are not destroyed by cutting down too many trees.

The Lungmanis Timber Camp has its own sawmill, where logs are processed and prepared for export as sawed timber. Most of Malaysia's sawed timber is exported to Europe, Japan, the U.S. and Australia.

My spare time is spent growing vegetables. Sometimes, when there is not much to do, I take a few days off to go into the forest to hunt. I hunt either wild pig or deer. My hunting dogs will sniff out the prey and then chase it. Once it is cornered, I kill it with my spear.

A kill means several days of free meat for my family and friends. Sometimes I set traps for the animals in the forest. Some hunters use guns but that's not for me. I prefer the good old-fashioned ways of my people.

Lumberjacks at Lungmanis are provided with homes built in the "longhouse" style of Sarawak.

"One of the world's busiest ports"

Denis Phillips is a Singaporean of English and Portuguese descent. He is a harbor pilot with the Port of Singapore Authority. The harbor is very busy, with a ship arriving or leaving every ten minutes.

I must have inherited my love of the sea from my English grandfather, who was a seafaring man. When I completed my schooling, I served a four-year apprenticeship before enrolling at the Singapore Polytechnic for a four-month course to get my Second Mate's overseas ticket. Then I worked for three years with various shipping companies.

As I love the sea and traveling, too, it was an excellent way of getting to see the world. I've been everywhere except to the United States and New Zealand.

When I got married and started a family, I switched to a shore-based job. I joined the Port of Singapore Authority and worked for six years as an assistant controller of shipping. But the call of the sea was too strong. So I went back on board ship, this time as a harbor pilot. I've been one for almost ten years now.

Singapore is one of the world's busiest ports. Situated at the crossroads of international trade routes, it has a well-sheltered, natural deep-water harbor which is navigable throughout the year. Singapore trades with nations all over the world. Supertankers, container ships, passenger liners, cargo freighters, bulk carriers, lighters, trawlers and coastal vessels flying the flags of almost all the maritime nations of the world, call at our port in the southern part of Singapore island.

The port operates around-the-clock throughout the year and is very busy. Every ten minutes, a ship either arrives or leaves. On any one day, you can see at least 600 ships in the harbor. More than 30,000 vessels call at the port every year. It also handles about 101 million tons of cargo annually.

All ships using the port are assured of a 24-hour tug and pilotage service. The Port of Singapore Authority employs about 100 harbor pilots who work nine-hour shifts.

When I get a call to bring a ship into port, I carry my two-way radio and take a launch out to sea. Once on board the ship, I am given charge of the vessel by the

Unloading containers is now a highly mechanized and computerized operation.

captain and am responsible for bringing it safely into port. Harbor pilots are necessary because they are familiar with the harbor, the tides, the currents, the force and direction of the wind and movement of ships in the area. They know the channels to use to avoid any dangerous reefs, shoals or wrecks, some of which are marked by buoys, beacons or lighthouses.

When the ship is safely berthed alongside the wharf or container terminal, its captain resumes command and I proceed to my next job.

Tugboats are used to help maneuver ships inside the harbor.

"The oil palm is Malaysia's golden crop now"

Jumadi bin Sarpani is an oil-palm harvester. He works on a plantation in Gelang Patah, 16 km (10 miles) northwest of Johore Bahru, capital of the state of Johore. He is 34, is married and has three children.

I've been working as an oil-palm harvester since 1975. On our plantation, 850 hectares (2,100 acres) of land is planted with oil palm, 728 hectares (1,800 acres) with rubber and 105 hectares (260 acres) with cocoa.

Most rubber plantations in Peninsular Malaysia are converting to oil palm. With remarkable increases in the price of palm oil, the oil palm is Malaysia's "golden crop" now. Unlike rubber, which takes about six to seven years to mature, the oil palm takes only about two-and-a-half years.

Labor requirements are not as high and the oil palm itself is a hardy crop that does not require much attention. It is therefore a better investment, with the result that 60 percent of the land in Malaysia is planted with oil palm, while the remaining 40 percent is planted with rubber.

I usually start work at 6:30 a.m. I work my way down the neat rows of oil palms. I use a strong, curved knife tied to a bamboo pole for harvesting the oil-palm fruit. The fruit consists of a large bunch of some 800 small, oval, reddish-black nuts. It grows among the fronds at the top of the palm. I have to cut off each frond before I can remove the fruit.

When the fruit drops to the ground, I use a spike to pierce and lift it into my wheelbarrow. This is because there are thorns on the fruit. When my wheelbarrow is full, I unload it at points along the track for collection by a truck.

I can harvest 2 hectares (5 acres) per day. By 1:30 p.m. my work is finished and I'm free for the rest of the day. I have an allocated area of 20 hectares (50 acres) to harvest. I usually take about ten days to harvest it.

I'm paid twice monthly, the payments being calculated per fresh fruit bunch I harvest. During a good crop, I can earn about M$600 to $700 (U.S.$250–$300) a month. When the crop is poor, my earnings drop to M$150 (U.S.$65) per month. I usually supplement my income by taking on other work on the plantation.

Our plantation does not process the oil-palm fruit; that's done by the people who

coastal plain, in the states of Perak, Selangor and Johore. The variety of oil palm that we grow produces fruits with thick, fleshy pericarps (soft outer coverings) and small kernels. Palm oil is therefore more important here than kernel oil.

Sabah produces palm oil, too. Malaysia is the world's largest producer of palm oil, supplying about 80 percent of its needs.

Fresh bunches of oil palm fruit are loaded onto a truck for delivery to a processing plant.

(Above) Long, neat rows of oil palms on the estate where Jumadi works, in the state of Johore.

buy our fruit. The oil-palm fruit must be processed quickly after picking because any delay affects the quality of the oil.

The palm oil is exported to countries like Singapore, India, Japan, Pakistan and the E.E.C. (European Economic Community). It is used for making edible oil, margarine, soap and candles.

The main areas where oil palm is grown in Peninsular Malaysia are on the western

"Singapore has many children of school-going age"

Harvinder Kaur is a schoolgirl in Singapore. She is 15 years old and is studying for her Singapore-Cambridge "O level" exams. She comes from a very traditional Sikh family.

I'm called Harvinder, which in Punjabi means goddess. Our tenth and last guru (religious teacher) said that as members of one family, all the Sikh men from the state of Punjab, in northern India, should be called "Singh" and all the women "Kaur." That's why my two brothers are

Gurwinder Singh and Jaswinder Singh, and I am Harvinder Kaur.

Like all traditional Sikh girls, I keep my hair long. I braid it to keep it neat and tidy. My brothers keep their hair long, too, according to our custom. They also wear turbans.

All three of us were born in Singapore and educated in English, which is the business language of the state. As my second language, I study Malay, the national language of our country. My other classmates study either Mandarin, Malay or Tamil, because the government encourages people to speak two languages. I haven't been taught Punjabi, but I've picked it up from my parents.

I go to the Katong Convent School. It's a Catholic school that accepts girls of all races and religions. All church schools are single-sex, whereas state schools are co-educational.

Harvinder and her classmates are preparing to take their "O-level" exams.

I'm studying for my "O levels" ("Ordinary Level" examinations taken at the age of 15 or 16). I've chosen to take English language, English literature, history, geography, biology, math and Malay. All students in Singapore take "O level" examinations.

I hope my results will be good enough for me to continue my studies and take the "A levels" (college entrance exams). I love children, and I'd like to become a teacher.

There are 42 girls in my class. We go to school in the mornings, from 7:30 a.m. to 1:00 p.m. The afternoon session is from 1:05 to 6:35 p.m. We've had two-session schools in Singapore for a very long time because of the large number of children of school-going age. But the number of children in Singapore is decreasing now because of the government's successful family planning campaign to "stop at two." Educational policies have changed, too. Slower students are allowed a longer time to complete their education.

On Sundays, my family goes to the *gurdwara* (Sikh temple) to worship. Most of our service consists of singing hymns. I'm learning to play the harmonium because I hope to be one of the musicians at the service.

During these occasions, my girlfriends and I wear our Punjabi dress. This consists of trousers and a knee-length tight-fitting blouse, called a *kameeze*. We have veils, too, for covering our heads during the service.

Although my parents are very traditional, they're not in the least bit old-fashioned. I'm allowed to go out with friends, attend parties, play games or go to concerts and plays. They don't mind as long as I tell them where I'm going. It makes me happy to know that I have their trust.

A class at Harvinder's school warms up before a gym class.

"Bintulu has changed beyond recognition"

Tajudin Ibrahim, 38, is an engineer with the Malaysia Liquefied Natural Gas (MLNG) plant near Bintulu, in Sarawak. Since the discovery of offshore gas, Bintulu has become a boom town.

I came to Bintulu in 1981 when the construction of the Malaysia Liquefied Natural Gas plant at Tanjung Kidurong, north of Bintulu, started. My job is to keep an eye on the contractors who are employed to make alterations to the plant. I have to make sure that the modifications run according to plan – in terms of time, money and safety.

Since coming here, I've had the opportunity of seeing Bintulu, a port and quiet little fishing village at the mouth of the Kemena River, change almost beyond recognition.

The wooden houses on stilts, facing the South China Sea, are still here. So are the market, where the fishermen bring in their catch, and the other wooden buildings in the older part of town. But overshadowing them are the hotels, the modern office buildings, supermarkets and related industries that have sprung up since the development of the gas plant, 19 km (12 miles) away.

Bintulu's population has grown five fold since the start of the eighties. The

Pipes carry the liquefied gas to the dock, where it is pumped into ships for export.

building industry is booming, especially in the housing projects along the main road between Bintulu and Tanjung Kidurong. You can't escape the dust as you walk around Bintulu, but I don't mind. This is an exciting place to live because out there in the South China Sea are our gasfields.

Undersea pipelines have been built to the gas plant from two gas fields 125 km (78 miles) offshore. The depth of the water in the area is about 71 m (233 feet). Another gas field, about 170 km (106 miles) offshore, is being planned.

The gas began flowing into our plant in 1982. It is processed and exported in liquefied form only to Japan at present. There, it is used as a fuel for industry and also for homes because it is much cleaner and cheaper than oil. We export the gas

Huge tanks for storing the liquefied gas produced at the plant where Tajudin works.

in a liquefied state because it takes up less space than if it were in a gaseous state. So it's cheaper to transport.

The gas plant is owned by PETRONAS (the National Oil Corporation of Malaysia), Shell and Mitsubishi. PETRONAS was formed in 1974 to take charge of the country's entire oil and natural gas resources.

As employees, we're given housing in a nearby development, where I live with my wife and two sons. During the weekends there's always the South China Sea to swim in or sailboard on. I play tennis and squash at our recreational club and when I go on vacation, there's always the whole of Sarawak for us to explore.

"Some longhouses have as many as 600 occupants"

Jampi anak Gamang, 41, is an Iban, people who were once known as the Sea Dayak. Some 26,000 Iban live on the island of Borneo. Jampi lives in Tutus in the state of Sarawak.

The question everyone asks when they come to our longhouse is: *"Berapa pintu?"* ("How many doors has it?")

Our longhouse, made mainly of wood, has 29 doors – one for each of the twenty-nine families living side-by-side in a seemingly endless row. Each family has its own "apartment" called a *bilek*. Iban longhouses can have any number of doors. They can grow, too, as extensions are made when space is needed for a growing family. Some longhouses have been known to have more than 80 doors, with as many as 600 occupants.

In front of our doors is a long, enclosed verandah which serves as a communal area. We call it a *ruai*. Here we store our sacks of rice, do our work, have our meetings, celebrate festivals or just sit and talk after work is done.

Beyond the *ruai* are platforms where we dry our rice or hang out our washing. Beneath our longhouse, which is built on stilts, live our pigs and poultry.

There are four other longhouses in Tutus, each connected to the other by raised, wooden walkways. Clusters of Iban longhouses are rather unusual except in the wet paddy-field area of the Rajang

A view of the longhouse at Tutus where Jampi is the tuai rumah.

River delta.

As a *tuai rumah* (head of a longhouse), I represent my community on any government matters. Sometimes, a family with a problem comes to me. I try my best to sort it out, but if things cannot be resolved, the matter is referred to the *penghulu* (chief of our district). If he cannot solve the problem, it's then taken to a court of law.

I've been a *tuai rumah* for three years now. My duties are mainly administrative and the state government pays me an allowance of M$200 (U.S.$84) a year.

All of us in Tutus are rice growers. Our fields are in the stretches of low, flat land behind our longhouses. We cultivate "wet" paddy fields, unlike the other Iban dwellers further upriver. They grow "dry" rice on the hillsides.

Our rice-growing season is between October and February. This is the wet season when the northeast monsoon blows. As the river overflows its banks during this time, we do not have any irrigation problems.

Harvesting starts at the end of February. If the harvest is good, we can earn money from the sale of the rice, which is our staple food.

Everyone helps out in the paddy fields, except the very young and the very old. When there's not much work to do, the men go out in their *prahus* (long narrow riverboats) to catch fish to eat or sell. Our womenfolk weave baskets, do beadwork or make hats and mats in their spare time. My wife, Ume, has a special loom to weave a red blanket with patterns of crocodiles, birds and frogs on it. We call it a *pua* and use it sometimes as a wall decoration on festive occasions.

Our most important festival is the *Dayak Gawai* which marks the end of the harvest and the beginning of the next planting season. It's celebrated on the first of June, a public holiday in Sarawak. There's dancing, singing, drinking and feasting, and celebrations often last a week in the longhouses along the rivers.

Another important occasion for us in Tutus is Christmas, because most of us are Christians. We have our own little Methodist Church which was built in 1965. A woman pastor comes by riverboat to conduct services for us every Sunday.

43

"Rivers are the highways of Sarawak"

Radin Sa'di is the skipper of the *Rajawali*. He plies up and down the River Rajang between Kapit and Sibu. A 25-year-old Malay, he recently married a Kenyah girl he met and fell in love with in Kapit, his hometown.

I was born in Kapit, a small rural town beside the Rajang, Sarawak's longest river. It's 272 km (170 miles) from the sea, in the heart of Iban country. My parents and grandparents were born here. Our ancestors came from Java in Indonesia.

Most of the people in Kapit are Chinese. As a result of growing up and going to an English school with my Chinese friends, I can speak *Hokkien*. It's the dialect of the main Chinese group here. Besides English and Malay, I can also speak Iban.

My wife, Livia Madan, is a Kenyah, one of the native people of Sarawak. Because I'm a Moslem, she has converted to Islam and is now known by her Moslem name, Sa'diah. I'm learning to speak the Kenyah language now.

I operate the *Rajawali*, an air-conditioned, fast riverboat that's equipped with a cassette tape recorder, radio and video recorder. It's been in operation for just a few months and is the second boat our company, a family-run business, owns. The other one, which isn't so well

equipped, is run by my eldest brother. We hope to buy a third boat in the near future.

My boat is 25.6 m (84 feet) long and 2.7 m (9 feet) wide. I had to pass a test to prove that I could handle it safely among all the rocks and shoals of the river. My operator's license has to be renewed every year.

Besides passengers, I also carry machinery and food for the lumber camps along my route. I have three employees on board. One is my assistant driver, while the other two help to collect fares, carry goods or steady the boat when passengers get on or off.

We leave Kapit at 9:00 a.m. and reach Sibu at about 1:30 p.m. We spend the night in Sibu and at 9:00 a.m. the next day, pick up our passengers and cargo and return to Kapit.

Ask anyone the distance between Kapit and Sibu, and you always get the answer, "About four to four-and-a-half hours." This is because on the Rajang and the other rivers of Sarawak, distance is always

The Rajawali *leaving Kapit to go down the Rajang River to Sibu.*

measured in time. I think Kapit and Sibu are about 128 km (80 miles) apart but even

I am not sure! The fare is M$13 (U.S.$5.00).

Our boats are expensive to run but business is good. We make a profit because in Sarawak, rivers are the highways of the country.

"Newspapers in the 4 official languages"

Tsang Sau Yin was born in Bombay, India. Her mother was from Malaysia and her father from Hong Kong. Brought up in Singapore, she now works as a journalist with *Business Times*, Singapore's English-language financial daily newspaper.

My mother came from Ipoh in Peninsular Malaysia. During World War II, when the Japanese army swept down the peninsula, her family fled south to Singapore. When it became obvious that Singapore, too, would be captured, they caught a ship to India.

In Bombay Mom met and married Dad, who had arrived earlier from Hong Kong. My brother was born in Bombay and so was I.

After the war, our parents brought us to Singapore. From school, I went on to the University of Singapore, now known as the National University of Singapore, to study sociology, history and political science. At the age of 21 I was given full Singapore citizenship.

Because of my interest in writing, meeting people and talking to them, I decided to make journalism my career. After graduation I became a reporter with a monthly business magazine.

I learned a lot on the job. I also took a three-month course at the School of Journalism to improve my interviewing and writing skills. Four years later I joined

The construction industry is one of the growth industries written about by Tsang Sau Yin.

Business Times.

You never get bored as a journalist. You meet many types of people, listen to different viewpoints and are always at the center of things.

I've been with *Business Times* for the past six years. The pace of work is fast and life can be rather hectic at times when there are deadlines to meet. *Business Times* caters to the business community of Singapore. Our paper focuses on local and overseas business news, finance and banking throughout the world, transportation, communications, management, property, shipping, company news as well as the Stock Exchange of Singapore. In the last ten years or so, Singapore has become an important financial center.

Small roadside stalls like this one sell everything from candy to local newspapers.

The newspapers in Singapore are in the four official languages of our multiracial society – English, Chinese, Malay and Tamil.

Our next-door neighbor, Malaysia, with a multiracial population not so very different from ours, has its own newspapers. About 60 newspapers are published in Malaysia. Like Singapore, its newspapers are in Malay, English, Chinese and Tamil. The Malay dailies have the largest circulation, with a combined circulation of some 660,000 copies, followed by the English-language papers.

"Sometimes I organize a *gotong royong*"

Dayang Jamayah has been a rural community worker with the Sarawak Federation of Women's Institutes for seven years. She lives in Kuching, the state capital of Sarawak, with her husband and their four children.

Home economics was my favorite subject in school. I was in my element when it came to planning a menu, counting food calories and organizing domestic science projects.

The skills I've learned are proving useful in my present job as a rural community worker. My work varies. Sometimes I keep regular office hours to do all my paperwork – letters, preparing courses, planning projects and organizing food fairs, and handicraft sales. At other times I travel around the *kampungs* (villages) in

Members of the Kuching branch of the Women's Institute work on their sewing project.

the five districts of Sarawak's First Division – Kuching, Bau, Lundu, Serian and Simunjan. The state of Sarawak is divided into divisions, which are sub-divided into districts.

There are meetings to attend, new branches of our Women's Institutes to open in the *kampungs* and projects to start up. Some of the rural projects include the planting of rice, corn, vegetables or bananas and the breeding of fish. The Sarawak Agricultural Department helps us with technical advice and materials.

The population of Sarawak is made up of Ibans (the largest native group in Sarawak), Chinese, Malays, Bidayuhs, Melanaus and the *Orang Ulu* minority groups – like the Kayans, Kenyahs, Kedayans, Muruts, Penans, Bisayas and Kelabits. *Orang Ulu* is a Malay term which means "People of the Interior." I'm a Malay in case you're wondering which group I belong to, although all of us think of ourselves as Malaysians now.

Most people in Sarawak are farmers, growing such things as pepper, rubber, sago, cocoa or coconuts on small holdings. On each, the women are involved in farm work as well as in running a home.

My job is to help rural women to improve their standards of living through community projects like child care, nutrition or home economics. Sometimes I organize a *gotong royong* where the people of the whole *kampung* come forward voluntarily to build their own community hall, waterpipes, drains or even toilets.

At present, the members of our Kuching branch of the Women's Institute are involved in a sewing project. We collect secondhand clothes, open the seams and re-use the material to make clothes for babies and young children.

These clothes will be sold very cheaply to members of our *kampung* branches and the money will go to our Kuching district fund. In this way we'll be helping the *kampung* mothers who are too busy tending their farms to sew clothes for their children, teaching our own Kuching members how to sew children's clothes and at the same time increasing our district funds. These funds are often used to help needy members of our branches.

Membership in our organization is open to all women, regardless of race, language or religion. It costs only M$1 (U.S. 42 cents) a year. Courses for members are usually held in our Kuching offices. One member from each of our 150 branches in the First Division is selected to attend the course. They then return to their communities to teach the other women. We reach a lot of rural women in this way, thus giving them an opportunity to learn and to improve their living conditions.

This kindergarten class is run by one branch of the Sarawak Women's Institute.

"The world's leading exporter of pepper"

Liew Toh Khian is a pepper farmer in the state of Sarawak. He is 29 and married, with five children. He works on the family farm in Serian, about 64 km (40 miles) from Kuching, the state capital. His ancestors were immigrants from China.

Sarawak, on the northwestern coast of the island of Borneo, has an area of 124,967 sq km (48,250 sq miles). It's about the size of Peninsular Malaysia and is the largest of Malaysia's thirteen states. For easier administration, it's divided into seven "divisions."

Pepper, a climbing plant that winds itself round hardwood poles, is grown mainly by Chinese farmers in Sarawak. The majority of these farms are only about 0.2 hectare (0.5 acre) in size, with each farmer having a wooden house on his land.

I've been helping out on the family farm since I was 8. So have my three brothers and five sisters. Our farm has an area of 1 hectare (2.5 acres). We've a total of 1,500 pepper vines. These are planted in straight rows, 2.4 m (8 feet) apart.

Planting usually takes place during the rainy season, which is from October to February. Young stem cuttings are planted on well-drained hillsides and allowed to grow for about five months. Then 3-meter (10-foot)-long hardwood poles are stuck into the earth to help support each growing vine.

The pepper vines take about two-and-a-half to three years to reach the top of each pole. They need careful cultivation. They're regularly weeded and fed with fertilizers—both natural and chemical ones.

Our vines are first harvested when they reach a height of 1.5 m (5 feet). The second harvest takes place when the vines reach their maximum height of 3 m (10 feet). Thereafter, they are harvested once a year usually during the hot, dry months of April to July when the tiny green berries begin to ripen. They turn red when ripe and have to be picked by hand.

The pepper berries are laid out on mats or plastic sheets and dried in the sun to produce black pepper. Some are soaked in water till the outer skin is removed. They are then dried to produce the more valuable white pepper.

The dried pepper is put into sacks and sold to dealers. They transport them to

Wooden rakes are used to spread out the white pepper to dry in the sun.

Kuching, where they're sold to pepper merchants who export them to Britain, the United States and the E.E.C. (European Economic Community).

In Kuching, 100 kg (220 lb) of black pepper can fetch about M$300 (U.S.$125), depending on its quality and the current market price. White pepper costs even more. Although pepper is an important crop, its price can fluctuate enormously.

Malaysia is the world's leading exporter of pepper. I've heard that in recent years we have been producing about 35,000 tons of it, 32,000 of which are exported.

A worker picking the clusters of tiny red berries which grow at the top of the pepper vine.

"Complete freedom of worship in Singapore"

Venerable Sek Bao Shi, 41, was a civil servant for 18 years before being ordained as a member of the *Mahayana* Buddhist Order in January, 1981. She is now a *Fa Shi*, or Buddhist novice, and hopes to receive her Higher Ordination soon.

It's 4:30 a.m. The sky is dark and it's rather cold, but I'm up and so are the other five members of our Buddhist Order. Only women live in our temple. By 5:00 a.m. we're chanting Buddhist *sutras* (scriptures) at our first service of the day.

At 7:00 a.m. we make our first offering of biscuits or bread and a cup of tea to Lord Buddha. A short service accompanies the offering. Then we have our breakfast of bread or oatmeal and a hot drink. We are vegetarians, because we don't believe in harming any living creature.

After breakfast, there are chores to do. These include cleaning, washing and preparing lunch. At 11:00 a.m., after the rice is cooked, we make a second offering to Lord Buddha. We have our lunch soon after and this is the final meal of the day.

To become a member of the Buddhist Order, it's customary to follow a Master or *Shi Fu* of one's choice for five years. When I decided to leave home, give up my job, rid myself of my worldly possessions, shave my head and devote myself to practicing Lord Buddha's teachings, I asked to be her disciple. I was very happy to be accepted. I have been my *Shi Fu's*

A young devotee, in her formal black robe, beats the drum during a service in the temple.

disciple for three years now.

My decision to join the Buddhist Order was not made overnight. I had been thinking about it since I was 9. As a child, I often accompanied my mother, a devout Buddhist, to the Kuan Yin Temple to make offerings to Kuan Yin, the Goddess of Mercy.

After completing my secondary schooling, I entered the civil service. Still deeply interested in the teachings of Lord Buddha, I became a vegetarian. As a lay devotee I went to The Buddhist Union Shrine to help out in religious and administrative activities. I also resolved to abstain from harming others, from stealing, from telling lies, from being unchaste and from all forms of intoxicating drinks and drugs. I spent seventeen years in this way until finally deciding to join the Buddhist Order at the age of 38.

Since then, I have been staying at the Leng Jin Temple to study the Buddhist scriptures with my *Shi Fu*. In addition, she teaches me how to meditate, conduct Buddhist services and beat the drum and cymbals during special ceremonies. I also have more than 500 rules to observe now.

I've found peace and happiness in the teachings of our Lord Buddha who said, "The gift of Truth excels all other gifts." I want to seek this Truth through the study of the Buddhist scriptures. I know it can be found within ourselves.

I am glad for the opportunity to practice what I believe in. There's complete freedom of worship in Singapore and wherever you go you will see temples, mosques, churches and other places of worship near to each other.

As a Buddhist, I'm very happy to see our people understanding and accepting one another's customs and religion. It makes for a much happier world.

Devotees worshipping at a Buddhist temple in Singapore.

"Malaysians are a sports-loving people"

M. Jegathesan is a doctor who lives in Petaling Jaya, in the state of Selangor. Once called the "fastest man in Asia," he has represented his country in world-class athletics.

I was raised on a diet of running. My father, who came to Malaysia from Sri Lanka, was a champion sprinter in the early 1920s. My three older brothers blazed their own trail after him and it was only natural that I, the youngest son, should follow the family tradition. I took to athletics like a duck to water.

Born in Kuala Kangsar, in the state of Perak, I began competing at elementary school – running away with all the prizes! When I was 12, my parents decided to send me to Singapore for my secondary schooling. I spent the next eleven years there, till I graduated as a doctor from the University of Singapore in 1967.

My athletic training began in earnest during my years in Singapore. My first international competition was in 1959 at the first SEAP (Southeast Asia Peninsular) Games in Bangkok. The following year, I took part in the Olympics at Rome. I was eliminated in the heats for the 400 meters, but I achieved my personal best time. So I returned to Singapore to train harder

than ever. I was only 16 then.

As a Malaysian citizen, I've represented Malaysia at all international competitions. I've competed in two Olympics, one Commonwealth Games, two Asian Games and three SEAP Games.

At the fifth Asian Games in 1966 I won the 100-meters sprint, to earn the title of "Fastest Man in Asia." I won the 200 meters, too, and helped the Malaysian team to victory in the 400 meters relay. What an experience!

We are a sports-loving people. We fill the stadiums to watch our favorite sports like soccer, badminton and hockey. We cheer our athletes and swimmers and take great pride in their achievements. Even traditional games like *wau* (kite-flying) and *gasing* (top-spinning) have a place in our society.

Soccer is the most popular sport in Malaysia today, but it's in badminton that this country has made its mark internationally.

Our population is made up of many

races. We speak many languages and come from different cultures, but in sports, our hearts and minds are one. There's great rejoicing when Malaysia wins and deep disappointment when we lose. Recognizing this unifying influence of sports on the people, our government has given it its full support.

Although I left the competitive field to concentrate on my medical career, my love of athletics has never waned. I've kept in touch with the techniques and trends and used my experience as a doctor and athlete to help our young, up-and-coming athletes.

As medical adviser to the Malaysian Amateur Athletic Union and President of the Malaysian Association of Sports Medicine, I advise various sporting associations on all medical aspects of sports. I give talks to athletes and their coaches and visit them when they're training for international competitions.

Malaysians are a sports-loving people. Popular sports include badminton and hockey.

Young Malaysian boys racing to beat the clock during a 100-meter sprint.

"Malaysia is a constitutional monarchy"

Rafidah Aziz is a Member of Parliament, and Minister of Public Enterprises. Married, with three children, she works in Kuala Lumpur, the capital of Malaysia, and lives on its outskirts.

I've been interested in politics since my college days. My first government post was as Parliamentary Secretary, then Deputy Minister of Finance and finally Minister of Public Enterprises.

Malaya, a federation of states, became

The Minister addresses a meeting in one of the villages in her constituency.

an independent country within the British Commonwealth in 1957, following an agreement between the British government and the rulers of the Malay states. In 1963, Sabah and Sarawak joined the federation, and the name of Malaysia was adopted. In 1965, Singapore left the federation to become an independent city-state.

It's a constitutional monarchy, with the

king, known as the *Yang Dipertuan Agung*, as the Supreme Head of State. A Sultan from one of the Malay states, he is elected by his fellow Sultans at the Conference of Rulers to hold office for five years. He acts on the advice of the Prime Minister and the Cabinet.

The Malaysian Parliament consists of the *Dewan Rakyat* (the House of Representatives) and the *Dewan Negara* (the Senate). The former has 154 members and is elected every five years. The latter has 68 members, 40 of whom are appointed by the King; the remainder being elected by the states.

Each state has its own constitution and government to handle its affairs. In Peninsular Malaysia, each state is divided into districts, run by a district officer. Each district is sub-divided into *mukims*, run by a chief called a *penghulu*. Sarawak is split up into divisions and Sabah into residencies.

Our Constitution sets out the broad outlines of how the country should be governed, establishing the rights of individuals and to what degree the government can limit them. The Constitution can be changed by Parliament if there is a two-thirds majority in favor of it.

As an MP (member of Parliament), I make myself available to the people of my constituency as often as possible. I meet them and talk to them and bring their problems to the attention of the relevant government departments. There are about 100,000 people in my constituency.

I've been the Minister of Public Enterprises since 1980. My ministry is in charge of 26 agencies, which run more than 500 companies. These companies are involved in all sorts of business – finance, shipping, mining, urban development, agriculture, tourism and the food industry.

My ministry does not supervise all public enterprises in the country, only a small number of them. In setting up this ministry, the government was aiming at improving the social and economic position of the Malays and native people of Malaysia by helping them participate in commerce and industry.

There's a lot of work to be done. We keep an eye on the performance of each agency, making sure that objectives are achieved, policies implemented and problem areas identified. I get regular reports on the agencies and I personally look into how they are run.

My official duties, Cabinet and committee meetings, functions, talks and meetings with my constituents and officials of the various agencies, keep me very busy. I don't have much free time. But I enjoy my work because I thrive on activity.

Computers in the Ministry of Public Enterprises in Kuala Lumpur keep records up to date.

Facts

Malaysia

Capital city: Kuala Lumpur.

Language: *Bahasa Malaysia* (Malay) is the national and official language. English is widely used in business. Other languages include Chinese dialects and Indian languages.

Currency: 1M$ (Malaysian dollar) = 100 cents and is worth 42 United States cents (summer 1984).

Religion: The official religion is Islam, but freedom of worship is guaranteed by the Constitution. Other major religions practiced are Buddhism, Taoism, Hinduism and Christianity.

Population: In 1982, there were 14,143,000 people in Malaysia, with 11,725,000 living in Peninsular Malaysia and 2,419,000 in Sabah and Sarawak. In Peninsular Malaysia, most people live in the western coastal area. About 45% of the population is under 45 years old.

Race: Malaysia has a diversity of races, the three main ones being (1) the Malays and other native groups like the Orang Asli of Peninsular Malaysia, the Kadazans and Bajaus of Sabah and the Ibans and Bidayuhs of Sarawak; (2) the Chinese; (3) the Indians.

Climate: An equatorial climate with rain and sunshine throughout the year. The northeast monsoon blows from October to February and the southeast monsoon from May to September. The average rainfall is about 254 cm (100 inches) a year. The average daily temperature varies from 21° to 32°C (70° to 90°F). Humidity is high.

Government: Malaysia is a federation of 13 states, each of which has its own constitution and government to handle state affairs. Malaysia is a constitutional monarchy. The *Yang Dipertuan Agung*, the king, is the supreme head of the federation. He is elected by the Conference of Rulers for 5 years. He acts on the advice of the Prime Minister and Cabinet, whom he appoints from members of the Parliament. This is made up of two houses, the Senate *(Dewan Negara)* and the House of Representatives *(Dewan Rakyat)*.

Education: In Peninsular Malaysia, 6 years of free elementary education and 5 years of secondary education are available to all children. Sabah and Sarawak have retained some independence in their teaching system, but it is very similar to that of Peninsular Malaysia. There are 5 universities and several colleges and technical institutes.

Agriculture: Mainly an agricultural country, Malaysia is the world's main producer of natural rubber, palm oil, tropical hardwood and pepper. Almost 50% of the workforce is involved in agriculture. More than 70% of Peninsular Malaysia and a large proportion of Sabah and Sarawak are covered by dense rain forest.

Industry: The economy is steadily being industrialized, and manufacturing industry is expanding rapidly. More than a third of the world's tin comes from Malaysia. Important industries include the processing of agricultural products, textiles, electronic equipment, chemicals, machinery and fertilizers. Most of Malaysia's trade is done with Japan, the United States and Singapore.

The Media: About 60 newspapers are published in Malaysia: in *Bahasa Malaysia*, English, Chinese and Tamil. They are all privately owned and have a high circulation.

Singapore

Capital city: Singapore City.

Languages: There are four official languages — English, Malay, Chinese (Mandarin), and Tamil. The national language is Malay and English is the business language. Most Singaporeans are bilingual.

Currency: 100 cents = 1 Singapore dollar, which is worth 46 United States cents (summer 1984).

Religion: There is complete religious freedom.

Population: In 1982, there were 2,472,000 people in Singapore, of whom 76.7% were Chinese, 14.7% were Malay, 6.4% were Indian, and 2.2% were of other races. About 60% of the people are under 30. The population is expanding rapidly, so the government is encouraging families to have only two children.

Race: The people of Singapore are of different ethnic origins, mainly descendants of immigrants from the Malay peninsula, China, India and Sri Lanka.

Climate: Equatorial, with high humidity and high rainfall. Temperatures vary between 24° and 30°C (75° to 86°F).

Government: Singapore became an independent city-state within the British Commonwealth in 1965. It is a republic with a one-chamber Parliament, made up of 75 members who are elected every 5 years. The President is the head of state, elected by Parliament for a 4-year term in office. There is a Prime Minister and a Cabinet.

Housing: Singapore enjoys a high standard of living with most families owning their own homes.

Education: Ten years of education is available to all children (6 years of elementary and 4 years of secondary), with an additional 2 years of pre-university education. Elementary education is free. Fees are nominal for secondary education; higher education is subsidized by the state. There is one university and several higher education and technical centers. Bilingualism is encouraged, with students learning English and their mother tongue.

Military service: National service is compulsory for all males when they reach the age of 18.

Agriculture: Less than 17% of the total land area is farmed. Farms are small and mainly used for pig and poultry farming, fruit and vegetable gardening, and growing orchids.

Industry: The port of Singapore is the largest in southeast Asia and the fourth largest in the world. Historically, Singapore's economy was based on the selling and distribution of goods from surrounding countries. This is still important – rubber, timber, pepper and petroleum products account for about 70% of the total trade – but in the last ten years the growth of manufacturing industries has been encouraged, including ship-building and repairing, iron and steel, textiles, footware, microelectronics, and scientific and medical instruments. Singapore has become an important financial center. Tourism is also a growth industry.

The Media: There are 10 daily newspapers in the 4 official languages, and one national radio and TV network.

Glossary

alluvium   Soil, sand, gravel, etc. carried by running water from higher ground and left on lower land.

batik   A process of printing patterns on fabric in which the parts not to be dyed are covered with wax.

frond   The leaf of a palm tree.

gambier   A vegetable dye used in tanning.

hydroponic farming   A way of growing plants in gravel, through which water containing fertilizers is pumped.

ingot   A lump of metal which has been shaped in a mold: gold ingots, for example.

lode   A deposit of a metal's ore in a rock.

opencast mining   Mining a mineral which is near the earth's surface, so there is no need for deep, underground tunnels.

paddy field   A field planted with rice.

sarung   A skirtlike garment, draped around the body, and worn by men and women.

rattan   Wickerwork or cane furniture.

shoal   Shallow, dangerous water in a river.

staple food   The main food in a person's or society's diet.

Acknowledgments

The pictures on pages 40 and 41 appear by courtesy of MLNG Sdn. Bhd., and the one on page 10 by courtesy of Charles K. K. Chua. The author and publishers would like to thank Malaysian Airline System for providing travel between Singapore and Malaysia and within Malaysia, and for the photographs on pages 28 and 29.

Index